AROHA TERESA

Moving Destiny

Dedicated to God

Contents

Preface

Moving Destiny follows the epic journey of three unlikely heroes—Elara Thornfield, a determined historian; Jareth, a skilled warrior with a hidden past; and Liora, an enigmatic archer with a mysterious connection to ancient magic. Their world is on the brink of chaos as dark forces, led by the malevolent sorcerer Malakar, threaten to upset the delicate balance between realms.

When ancient artifacts of immense power are discovered—The Orb of Insight, The Crown of Harmony, and The Scepter of Valor—the trio is thrust into a perilous quest to unlock the Gate of Aetheria, a mythical portal that holds the key to restoring balance and saving their world. Their journey takes them through treacherous landscapes, enchanted realms, and the ominous Obsidian Citadel.

As they confront formidable foes, solve ancient riddles, and navigate shifting alliances, Elara, Jareth, and Liora must rely on their unique strengths and forge unbreakable bonds of trust. Each artifact they possess brings them closer to their ultimate goal, but it is their courage and unity that will determine the fate of their world.

In the climactic final battle against Malakar, the trio faces their greatest challenge yet. With the balance of the realms hanging in the balance, they must harness the full power of the artifacts to overcome darkness and bring about a new era of peace.

Moving Destiny is a tale of adventure, sacrifice, and the transformative power of unity. It explores themes of destiny, friendship, and the enduring struggle between light and darkness, culminating in a story where the future of many worlds rests on the courage of a few.

Acknowledgement

Thanks for your support

1

The Call to Adventure

Certainly! Here is a full-text e

Chapter 1: The Call to Adventure

In the quiet village of Evershade, nestled between rolling hills and dense forests, life moved with the steady rhythm of the seasons. For most of its residents, the days blended into one another, marked only by the changing colors of the leaves and the shifting patterns of the clouds. Among these villagers lived Elara Thornfield, a young woman whose presence was as unremarkable as the village itself. She had a routine—wake up with the sunrise, tend to the garden, help at the local inn, and retire with the sunset. But for all its tranquility, her life felt incomplete, as though an unspoken yearning lingered just beyond her grasp.

Elara's father, Cedric Thornfield, was a respected blacksmith, his hands calloused from years of shaping metal. He was a pillar of the community, known for his kindness and skill. Her mother,

Lyra, had passed away when Elara was very young, leaving behind only memories and a locket that Elara cherished dearly. Cedric's attempts to fill the void left by Lyra were earnest, but the loss had woven an invisible thread of sadness into their lives.

One crisp autumn morning, as the sun painted the sky in hues of gold and orange, Elara set out on her usual walk through the village square. The leaves crunched beneath her boots, and a gentle breeze whispered through the trees. As she passed the old well at the center of the square, she noticed something unusual: a figure clad in a dark cloak, standing near the edge of the village. The figure's face was obscured, but there was an unmistakable air of purpose about them.

Elara hesitated for a moment, her curiosity piqued. The figure seemed out of place, their presence a stark contrast to the familiar comfort of Evershade. Gathering her courage, she approached the cloaked stranger.

"Good morning," Elara said, her voice steady despite her apprehension. "Can I help you with something?"

The figure turned, revealing a face marked by age and wisdom. His eyes, a deep shade of green, seemed to hold secrets of distant lands and forgotten tales. "You must be Elara Thornfield," the stranger said, his voice a soft, resonant baritone.

Elara's eyes widened. "Yes, that's me. But how do you know my name?"

The stranger smiled faintly. "There are many things in this

world that are known to those who listen closely. I have come with a message for you, one that will alter the course of your life."

Elara's heart raced. "What kind of message?"

The stranger reached into his cloak and produced a small, intricately carved wooden box. He held it out to Elara, who took it with trembling hands. The box was cool to the touch and adorned with symbols she did not recognize.

"This box," the stranger explained, "contains a map and a key. The map will guide you to a place of great significance, and the key will unlock a path that has long been hidden. You are destined to find something that has been lost for generations."

Elara's mind whirled with questions. "Why me? I'm just a simple village girl. What could I possibly have to do with such a journey?"

The stranger's gaze softened. "Sometimes, it is the seemingly ordinary who are chosen for extraordinary tasks. The strength you seek is within you, waiting to be discovered."

Before Elara could respond, the stranger turned and walked away, vanishing into the mist that was beginning to roll in from the forest. Elara stood there, the weight of the box heavy in her hands, her mind a tumult of thoughts and emotions.

As she returned home, the box felt like a tangible promise of change. She knew that whatever lay ahead would be far from the life she had known. The quiet village of Evershade seemed suddenly smaller, its familiarity giving way to the thrilling unknown that beckoned beyond its borders.

Elara's journey was about to begin, and the call to adventure had never been clearer.

— -

Feel free to adjust the chapter

2

Crossing the Threshold

Elara Thornfield stood on the edge of Evershade, the wooden box clutched tightly in her hands. The village had receded into the distance, and the familiar landscape of rolling hills and well-tended gardens gave way to a sprawling wilderness that seemed to stretch endlessly before her. The decision to leave was both exhilarating and terrifying, the comfort of her old life slipping away with each step she took.

The morning fog had lifted, revealing a path that wound through the dense forest. Tall trees with ancient, gnarled branches arched overhead, their leaves whispering secrets in the breeze. Elara had never ventured far from the village, and the prospect of traversing this uncharted territory filled her with a mixture of dread and anticipation.

As she began her journey, the map from the wooden box guided her. It was a delicate parchment with cryptic symbols and a winding route marked in faded ink. Elara spread it out on the ground, studying it carefully before tucking it into her satchel. The key, a small ornate piece of metal, was safely secured around her neck on a chain. It felt heavy, but it also reminded her of the purpose that lay ahead.

The forest path was both beautiful and daunting. Sunlight filtered through the canopy, casting dappled shadows on the forest floor. Every sound—a rustling leaf, a distant birdcall— seemed amplified in the quiet of the woods. The air was crisp and cool, carrying the earthy scent of damp soil and pine. Despite the tranquility, Elara's senses were heightened, every crack of a twig or flutter of a bird's wing causing her to jump slightly.

Hours passed as she walked, her progress marked by the occasional clearing that offered brief respite. She encountered a small stream, its clear waters sparkling in the sunlight. Elara knelt to drink, her reflection rippling in the current. She wondered about the journey ahead and the mysteries that awaited her. The tranquil beauty of the forest was both a comfort and a reminder of how far she had strayed from the life she knew.

As dusk approached, the forest began to change. Shadows lengthened, and the once-friendly path seemed to grow more ominous. The trees, now silhouetted against the darkening sky, loomed like silent sentinels. Elara quickened her pace, the distant promise of a campsite she had spotted on the map urging her forward.

Just as the last light of day faded, she reached a small, overgrown clearing with a single, ancient oak tree at its center. At the base of the tree, partially hidden by underbrush, was a weathered stone archway, covered in vines and moss. Elara's heart raced as she approached. This must be the place marked on the map.

With trembling hands, she took out the key and examined the archway. There was a lock set into the stone, its intricate design matching the key she carried. Elara inserted the key, turning it slowly. The lock clicked, and the archway creaked open, revealing a hidden passageway.

The passage was dimly lit by the faint glow of bioluminescent fungi growing on the walls. Elara took a deep breath and stepped through the archway, the cool air of the underground space wrapping around her like a shroud. The tunnel seemed to stretch on endlessly, the stone walls glistening with moisture.

As she ventured deeper, the sounds of the forest faded away, replaced by the steady drip of water and the occasional distant echo. Elara's mind was filled with a whirlwind of thoughts— her father's worried face, the life she had left behind, and the uncertainty of what lay ahead. But with each step, she felt a growing sense of determination. The threshold had been crossed, and there was no turning back now.

The passageway finally opened into a vast underground chamber, illuminated by a soft, ethereal light that seemed to emanate from the very walls. In the center of the chamber was a pedestal, upon which rested an ancient tome bound in ornate leather. The sight of the book filled Elara with a sense of awe and reverence. This was the beginning of something profound, a journey that would test her in ways she could scarcely imagine.

As Elara approached the pedestal, she knew that her life had irrevocably changed. The call to adventure had led her to this moment, and the path ahead was filled with both uncertainty and promise. With a deep breath, she reached out to take the tome, ready to face whatever trials and discoveries awaited her on this extraordinary journey.

3

Allies and Enemies

The underground chamber was vast and silent, save for the soft hum of the glowing fungi that bathed the room in an otherworldly light. Elara Thornfield stood before the pedestal, her fingers hovering above the ancient tome that rested there. The air was thick with the weight of history, and every shadow seemed to hide secrets waiting to be uncovered.

As she reached for the tome, a sudden noise startled her—a low, menacing growl echoed through the chamber. Elara spun around, her heart pounding in her chest. Emerging from the shadows was a creature unlike any she had ever seen. It was large, with dark fur and piercing red eyes that glowed ominously in the dim light. Its presence was intimidating, and its growl was a clear warning that Elara was not alone.

Instinctively, Elara stepped back, her eyes darting around for any sign of escape. But before she could react further, a figure leaped into the chamber, moving with surprising speed and grace. Clad in a dark cloak and armed with a slender sword, the newcomer engaged the creature with precision and skill. The clash of steel against claws echoed through the chamber as the two battled fiercely.

Elara watched in awe and fear as the figure fought. The stranger's movements were fluid and controlled, each strike delivered with practiced ease. After a tense few moments, the creature let out a final, anguished howl before collapsing to the ground, its life extinguished.

Breathing heavily, the figure sheathed their sword and turned to Elara. The hood of their cloak was pulled back to reveal a young man with sharp features and an air of quiet confidence. His eyes, a piercing blue, met Elara's with a mix of curiosity and wariness.

"Are you alright?" the young man asked, his voice calm but with an edge of urgency.

Elara nodded, still in shock. "Yes, I think so. Thank you. I didn't expect to encounter anything like that."

The young man's gaze softened slightly. "The creatures in these parts are not to be taken lightly. I'm Jareth, by the way. And you must be the one the legends spoke of."

Elara frowned. "Legends? I'm not sure what you mean."

Jareth's expression grew serious. "I've been searching for

someone who would be able to undertake the task ahead. There are ancient prophecies about a chosen one who would unlock the secrets of the hidden realms. I believe that person is you."

Before Elara could ask more, another figure emerged from the shadows. This new arrival was a woman, dressed in practical clothing with a bow slung across her back. Her eyes were sharp and assessing, and she moved with a fluid grace that suggested she was skilled in combat.

"Jareth," the woman said, her tone cool and composed. "I see you've made contact. I'm Liora. We've been following the same trail, and it seems our paths have finally crossed."

Jareth nodded in acknowledgment. "Liora, this is Elara Thorn-field. She has the tome that we need."

Liora's eyes widened slightly as she looked at Elara. "You found it. Good. We've been searching for a key to unlocking the ancient gate."

Elara felt a surge of confusion. "Unlocking a gate? What are you talking about?"

Liora approached, her demeanor shifting to one of earnestness. "There are forces at play that you need to understand. The tome you have is one part of an ancient puzzle. It holds the knowledge needed to access the Gate of Aetheria, a powerful artifact that can alter the balance of our world."

Jareth added, "And there are those who would use it for their own ends. We need to find the gate before they do."

Elara glanced between Jareth and Liora, realizing the gravity of the situation. "And how do I fit into all of this?"

Liora took a deep breath. "You've been chosen because the legends speak of someone who has the heart and courage to face the trials ahead. You have a role to play, and we need to work together to ensure that the gate is protected from those who would misuse it."

Jareth's expression softened. "It won't be easy. There will be dangers and challenges, but you won't be alone. We will be with you every step of the way."

As the realization of the journey ahead settled in, Elara felt a mix of apprehension and resolve. She had crossed the threshold into a world far more complex and dangerous than she had ever imagined. But with allies like Jareth and Liora by her side, she felt a glimmer of hope.

The chamber, now cleared of immediate danger, seemed to hold a promise of new beginnings. Elara took a deep breath, steeling herself for the trials that lay ahead. With her new companions, she was ready to face whatever came next, knowing that the path would be fraught with both allies and enemies, each playing a crucial role in the unfolding saga.

4

The Road of Trials

Elara Thornfield's journey had only just begun, and already, the challenges ahead seemed daunting. The ancient tome she carried had led her to Jareth and Liora, two allies who had quickly become indispensable. Together, they set out from the underground chamber, ready to face whatever lay on the road of trials that awaited them.

The path ahead was treacherous, winding through dense forests and across rugged terrain. The map indicated several key locations they needed to reach, each marked by ancient symbols and cryptic notes. According to Jareth, each location represented a trial they would need to overcome in order to unlock the secrets of the Gate of Aetheria.

The first trial was located in the Whispering Woods, a place known for its magical properties and elusive creatures. As they entered the forest, Elara marveled at the vibrant colors of the foliage and the ethereal glow of the luminescent plants that lined their path. But the beauty of the woods was deceptive; the air was thick with enchantments that made it difficult to discern reality from illusion.

Jareth led the way, his keen senses alert to every rustle and whisper. Liora followed closely, her eyes scanning the surroundings for any signs of danger. Elara, carrying the tome, felt both a sense of awe and trepidation. She was acutely aware that this was only the beginning of their journey, and each trial would test her in ways she could scarcely imagine.

As they ventured deeper into the woods, the air grew colder, and the forest seemed to close in around them. The path became less distinct, obscured by mist and shadow. It was then that they encountered the first of many obstacles—a series of enchanted riddles etched into ancient stones that blocked their way.

Jareth approached the stones, studying the inscriptions. "These riddles are meant to test our wit and resolve. We must solve them to proceed."

Elara looked at the inscriptions, which glowed faintly with magical energy. They were written in an archaic script that she struggled to decipher. Liora, however, had a sharp mind for puzzles and quickly began to analyze the riddles.

With Liora's guidance, they worked together to solve the riddles. Each correct answer caused the stones to shift and reveal a new part of the path. The process was both mentally exhausting and exhilarating, and Elara could feel the weight of their task pressing down on her. But with each success, their confidence grew.

After hours of navigating through the riddles, they finally emerged from the Whispering Woods and found themselves at the base of a steep mountain range. The second trial was known as the Trial of Endurance, and it would require them to climb the treacherous peaks to retrieve a crystal from the summit.

The climb was grueling. The mountain paths were narrow and perilous, with sheer cliffs and loose rocks making every step a challenge. The higher they climbed, the harsher the elements became. Snow and ice coated the rocks, and the wind howled with an unrelenting fury.

Elara struggled with the climb, her strength waning as the altitude and cold took their toll. Jareth and Liora, however, were seasoned travelers and provided support and encouragement. They took turns leading the way, their skills and experience proving invaluable.

Despite the physical strain, Elara pushed forward, determined to reach the summit. The trials were testing her resolve and endurance, but she refused to give up. The summit seemed to be an endless distance away, but with each grueling step, she could see the peak coming closer.

Finally, they reached the summit, where they found a crystal embedded in a stone pedestal. The crystal glowed with an inner light, and Elara felt a surge of triumph as she approached it. With the crystal in hand, they began their descent, the challenges they faced on the mountain etched into their memories.

As they made their way down, exhausted but victorious, Elara reflected on the trials they had overcome. Each challenge had tested her in different ways, pushing her to her limits both mentally and physically. Yet, with each trial, she felt a growing sense of strength and resilience.

By the time they reached the base of the mountain, night had fallen, and the stars sparkled in the clear sky above. They set up camp, their bodies aching but their spirits high. As they gathered around the fire, Elara knew that their journey was far from over. More trials lay ahead, each promising its own set of challenges and discoveries.

The road of trials was not just a path to the Gate of Aetheria but a journey of self-discovery and growth. Elara had begun to understand the depth of her own courage and the importance of her allies. The path ahead remained uncertain, but with each step, she was one step closer to unlocking the secrets that awaited them.

As the fire crackled and the night settled in, Elara looked at her companions with renewed determination. The trials they had faced had only strengthened their resolve, and together, they would continue their quest, ready to confront whatever challenges lay on the road of trials.

— -

Feel free to adjust or expand upon this chapter as needed for your story!

5

The Mentor's Wisdom

Certainly! Here is a full-text example of Chapter 5 titled "The Mentor's Wisdom":

—-

Chapter 5: The Mentor's Wisdom

The dawn light filtered through the canopy of the dense forest as Elara Thornfield, Jareth, and Liora continued their journey. The trials they had faced had been demanding, but the road ahead was fraught with even greater uncertainty. Their quest to uncover the secrets of the Gate of Aetheria had led them to a crucial juncture: they needed guidance from someone who possessed the knowledge and experience to help them navigate the challenges that lay ahead.

According to the ancient tome, their next destination was a secluded hermitage deep within the heart of the Enchanted Forest. This hermitage was reputed to be the home of an enigmatic figure known only as the Sage of the Woods, a mentor who was said to have unparalleled wisdom and insight into the arcane.

As they trekked through the forest, the landscape began to change. The trees grew larger and more ancient, their gnarled branches forming intricate patterns against the sky. The air was filled with the sweet scent of blooming flowers and the gentle hum of magical creatures. It was clear they were entering a place of profound enchantment.

After hours of hiking, they arrived at a clearing where a modest yet elegant cottage stood nestled among the trees. The cottage was built from natural materials, its walls adorned with ivy and its roof covered in moss. A gentle plume of smoke rose from the chimney, suggesting warmth and comfort within.

Elara felt a mix of anticipation and nervousness as they approached the cottage. Jareth and Liora, though composed, shared her sense of urgency. They had heard tales of the Sage's wisdom but had no idea what to expect from this meeting.

The door to the cottage creaked open, and an elderly figure appeared in the doorway. The Sage of the Woods was a tall, wiry man with a long white beard and a serene, knowing expression. He wore robes woven from leaves and vines, and his eyes sparkled with an otherworldly light.

"Welcome, travelers," the Sage said, his voice warm and inviting. "I have been expecting you."

Elara stepped forward, feeling a mixture of awe and relief. "We seek your guidance, Sage. We are on a quest to uncover the secrets of the Gate of Aetheria and need your wisdom to proceed."

The Sage nodded, his gaze penetrating yet kind. "The path you have chosen is fraught with peril, but it is also one of great significance. The Gate of Aetheria holds the power to shape the fate of many worlds, and only those with true resolve and understanding can unlock its secrets."

He motioned for them to enter the cottage, and they stepped inside. The interior was cozy, filled with the warm glow of candles and the aroma of herbs and incense. Shelves lined the walls, filled with ancient tomes, mystical artifacts, and curious trinkets.

The Sage gestured for them to sit at a circular wooden table in the center of the room. "Tell me what you have learned so far," he said, settling into a chair opposite them.

Jareth took out the tome and placed it on the table. "We have faced several trials, including solving riddles in the Whispering Woods and retrieving a crystal from the summit of the Trial of Endurance. Each challenge has tested our skills and resolve."

The Sage examined the tome with a thoughtful expression. "The trials you have faced are designed to prepare you for the ultimate challenge. The Gate of Aetheria is not just a physical barrier but a manifestation of ancient magic that requires both strength and wisdom to unlock."

He paused, his eyes meeting each of theirs in turn. "To succeed, you must understand the nature of the gate and the forces that seek to control it. There are dark entities that desire its power for themselves, and they will stop at nothing to achieve their goals."

Liora, ever perceptive, spoke up. "What can we do to protect the gate and ensure it is used for good?"

The Sage's expression grew serious. "You must seek out the remaining artifacts needed to unlock the gate. Each artifact represents a different aspect of the gate's power and must be used in harmony. You will need to find the Orb of Insight, the Crown of Harmony, and the Scepter of Valor. Only when these artifacts are united will you be able to access the true power of the gate."

Elara listened intently, absorbing the gravity of the Sage's words. "Where can we find these artifacts?"

The Sage nodded toward a large map hanging on the wall. "The locations of the artifacts are marked on this map. However, each location is protected by its own set of challenges and guardians. You will need to use all of your skills and knowledge to overcome these obstacles."

He then reached into a drawer and produced a small, intricately carved box. "This is the Box of Foresight. It will help you in your journey by revealing glimpses of what lies ahead. Use it wisely, for it can provide valuable insights but also reveal what you are not yet ready to face."

Elara accepted the box with a sense of reverence. "Thank you, Sage. We will do our best to honor the task before us."

The Sage smiled, his eyes twinkling with approval. "Remember, the journey is as important as the destination. Trust in yourselves and in each other. Your courage and wisdom will be your greatest allies."

With their guidance and the Box of Foresight in hand, Elara, Jareth, and Liora prepared to leave the Sage's hermitage. The wisdom they had gained would be crucial as they continued their quest. The path to the Gate of Aetheria was still fraught with challenges, but with the knowledge and artifacts they sought, they felt better equipped to face the trials ahead.

As they stepped back into the forest, the weight of their responsibility was tempered by a renewed sense of purpose. The road ahead was uncertain, but with the Sage's wisdom guiding them, they were ready to confront whatever lay in their path.

— -

Feel free to modify or expand

6

The Abyss

Certainly! Here is a full-text example of Chapter 6 tit
   The Abyss

The journey to find the remaining artifacts had taken Elara Thornfield, Jareth, and Liora across treacherous landscapes and through daunting challenges. Their path led them now to the Edge of the Abyss, a place shrouded in darkness and foreboding, known to be the home of the final trial before they could obtain the Orb of Insight.

The Abyss was not a physical location but rather a realm of shadow and illusion, a void that existed between the material world and the mystical dimensions. The entrance was a jagged chasm, flanked by towering cliffs that loomed like silent sentinels. A chilling wind howled through the ravine, carrying with it whispers that seemed to echo from the depths of the earth.

Elara stood at the precipice, her heart pounding. The abyss was said to prey on one's deepest fears and insecurities, making it a place where many had failed to return. She felt a cold shiver run down her spine, but she steeled herself, knowing that she had come too far to turn back now.

Jareth, ever the pragmatist, checked their supplies and ensured that their gear was secure. Liora, her expression grim, scanned the area for any signs of danger. The three of them had prepared for this moment, but the reality of facing the abyss was more daunting than they had anticipated.

"Remember," Jareth said, his voice steady despite the foreboding atmosphere, "the Abyss tests not just your strength but your resolve and clarity of mind. We must face our fears head-on if we are to succeed."

Elara nodded, her grip tightening on the Box of Foresight, which they had been using to guide their journey. The box had remained inert for the past few days, but as they neared the abyss, it began to emit a faint, pulsing glow. The artifact seemed to sense the gravity of their situation.

With a deep breath, Elara led the way, stepping cautiously toward the chasm. The ground beneath them was uneven, and each step seemed to echo with an eerie resonance. The darkness of the abyss seemed to swallow all light, creating an oppressive sense of unease.

As they descended into the chasm, the temperature dropped sharply. The darkness seemed to close in around them, and the whispers grew louder, becoming a cacophony of haunting voices. Elara could not distinguish individual words but felt the emotions behind them—fear, regret, and sorrow.

Suddenly, a figure materialized from the darkness—a manifestation of Elara's deepest fears. It was a shadowy form that mirrored her own appearance but was twisted into a grotesque semblance of her insecurities and doubts. The figure's eyes glowed with a malevolent light, and its voice was a distorted echo of her own.

"Do you really believe you are worthy?" the shadow hissed. "You're just a village girl. You don't have the strength to face what lies ahead."

Elara's breath caught in her throat. The shadow's words struck a deep chord, dredging up the self-doubt she had tried to suppress. But she knew that succumbing to fear was not an option. Gathering her courage, she focused on the words of the Sage and the support of her companions.

Jareth and Liora stepped forward, confronting their own fears. Jareth faced a vision of failure and inadequacy, while Liora grappled with a manifestation of her past mistakes and regrets. Each of them fought against their fears, their resolve strengthened by the bond they shared and the purpose that drove them.

Elara took a deep breath, finding strength in the presence of her allies. She reached deep within herself, confronting the shadow that loomed before her. "I may have doubts, but I have come this far because I believe in something greater than myself. I believe in our cause and in the strength we find together."

The shadow wavered, its form flickering as if struggling to maintain its shape. With a final surge of determination, Elara reached out and touched the shadow. As her hand made contact, the darkness began to dissolve, and the figure dissipated into nothingness.

With the manifestation of her fear vanquished, Elara felt a surge of relief. The oppressive darkness of the abyss seemed to lift slightly, revealing a path that led deeper into the chasm. The way forward was illuminated by a faint, otherworldly light that emanated from the depths.

The trio continued along the path, their progress marked by a newfound sense of determination. The abyss had tested their will and resolve, but they had emerged stronger and more united. As they approached the heart of the chasm, they could see the Orb of Insight—a brilliant, pulsating sphere—suspended in a field of shimmering light.

Elara reached out and carefully retrieved the orb, feeling its energy resonate with her own. The darkness of the abyss seemed to recede, replaced by a sense of accomplishment and clarity. The trial had been a formidable challenge, but they had succeeded.

With the Orb of Insight in hand, Elara, Jareth, and Liora emerged from the abyss, their spirits buoyed by their victory. The journey ahead would undoubtedly present more challenges, but they were ready to face them, fortified by the wisdom and strength they had gained.

As they left the chasm behind, the landscape began to change, and the path to their next destination came into view. The road of trials had brought them to this point, and the trials they had faced had prepared them for the final leg of their quest. With the Orb of Insight and their resolve strengthened, they pressed onward, ready to confront whatever lay ahead.

7

The Trial of Echoes

The journey from the Edge of the Abyss had been long and arduous, but with the Orb of Insight now safely in their possession, Elara Thornfield, Jareth, and Liora felt a renewed sense of purpose. Their next objective was clear: retrieve the Crown of Harmony. The clues in the ancient tome had led them to a remote mountain range known as the Veil of Echoes, where the trial to obtain the crown awaited.

The Veil of Echoes was notorious for its unsettling phenomena—sound seemed to reverberate endlessly, creating an atmosphere of confusion and disorientation. The mountain range was shrouded in mist, and the echoes of the environment played tricks on the senses, making navigation a challenge.

As they approached the base of the mountains, the mist thickened, obscuring their view. The path ahead was barely discernible, and the echoes of their footsteps seemed to bounce back at them, creating an eerie, repetitive soundscape.

"We must remain focused," Jareth said, his voice cutting through the disorienting echoes. "The trial of echoes is not just about finding the crown; it's about overcoming the confusion that the mountain creates."

Elara nodded, gripping the Orb of Insight tightly. The orb's faint glow provided some guidance, but the echoes made it difficult to pinpoint the direction. As they ventured deeper into the mist, the environment became increasingly surreal. The echoes of their voices mingled with phantom sounds—distant conversations, footsteps, and even haunting melodies—that seemed to come from nowhere and everywhere at once.

Liora, her sharp instincts alert, suggested they use the orb to help navigate. "The orb should help us discern the true path from the illusions created by the echoes. Let's stay close and use it to guide us."

They pressed on, relying on the orb's guidance. The echoes grew more intense, creating a cacophony of overlapping sounds. Elara found herself increasingly disoriented, her sense of direction compromised by the endless reverberations. At times, the echoes seemed to form coherent phrases, whispering doubts and fears that made her question their mission.

"Are you sure this is the right way?" an echo of her own voice seemed to question. "What if we're lost?"

Elara shook her head, trying to silence the echoing doubts. "We have to trust in our purpose and the wisdom we've gained."

Their progress was slow, but the Orb of Insight began to emit a stronger, more focused light, cutting through the mist and guiding them toward a hidden passage. As they followed the orb's lead, the echoes grew quieter, their path becoming clearer.

After what felt like hours of navigating through the shifting echoes, they arrived at a large cavern, its entrance concealed by a waterfall cascading down from the mountain. The sound of the waterfall created a powerful echo, masking the true entrance to the cavern.

Jareth examined the area and spotted a narrow crevice behind the waterfall. "We need to find a way to get past this. The entrance should be behind the waterfall."

With some effort, they squeezed through the crevice, emerging into the cavern. Inside, the echoes were replaced by a profound silence, broken only by the occasional drip of water. The cavern was vast, with walls adorned in ancient symbols and illuminated by the soft glow of bioluminescent fungi.

At the center of the cavern stood a pedestal, upon which rested the Crown of Harmony. The crown was a magnificent artifact, adorned with intricate designs and sparkling gemstones. Its presence seemed to fill the cavern with a harmonious resonance.

Elara approached the pedestal cautiously. "This must be the crown we've been seeking. But there may be more to this trial."

As she reached out to take the crown, the cavern's silence was shattered by a sudden, deafening roar. The echoes returned with a vengeance, more chaotic and disorienting than before. The walls of the cavern seemed to close in, and the echoes took on a menacing tone, as if challenging their right to claim the crown.

Jareth drew his sword, ready to confront any threats. Liora nocked an arrow, her senses on high alert. Elara, feeling the weight of their task, tried to focus on the crown, using the Orb of Insight to cut through the disorienting echoes.

The echoes grew louder, forming a swirling vortex of sound that threatened to overwhelm them. Elara concentrated on the orb, which began to emit a powerful beam of light. The light cut through the chaotic echoes, revealing a path through the tumultuous soundscape.

With a final surge of determination, Elara reached the pedestal and claimed the Crown of Harmony. As she lifted the crown, the echoes began to dissipate, and the cavern returned to its serene silence. The harmonious resonance of the crown seemed to stabilize the environment, bringing calm and clarity.

Exhausted but victorious, Elara, Jareth, and Liora made their way out of the cavern. The Veil of Echoes had tested their ability to navigate through confusion and doubt, but they had succeeded in overcoming the trial. The Crown of Harmony was a symbol of their perseverance and unity.

As they emerged from the mountain range, the mist began to clear, revealing the path to their next destination. With the

Crown of Harmony secured and their resolve strengthened, they were ready to face whatever challenges lay ahead on their quest for the final artifact.

The journey had been arduous, but each trial had brought them closer to their goal. With the wisdom and artifacts they had gathered, Elara, Jareth, and Liora pressed onward, their spirits buoyed by their accomplishments and their determination unwavering.

8

The Hidden Sanctuary

With the Crown of Harmony secured, Elara Thornfield, Jareth, and Liora pressed onward in their quest to find the final artifact: the Scepter of Valor. The ancient tome had provided them with a new clue—the scepter was hidden in a place known as the Hidden Sanctuary, a legendary realm that was said to be concealed from the ordinary eye and accessible only to those who proved themselves worthy.

The path to the Hidden Sanctuary was not marked on any map. The clue had led them to a remote, uncharted region known as the Whispering Glades, a mystical forest known for its illusionary magic and deceptive beauty. The glades were said to be alive with enchantments, where reality was often blurred with illusion.

As they entered the Whispering Glades, the landscape seemed to shift and change with every step. The trees were tall and ancient, their leaves shimmering with a kaleidoscope of colors that shifted unpredictably. The air was filled with a sweet, intoxicating fragrance, and the sounds of the forest created a melody that seemed both familiar and alien.

"This place is more disorienting than I imagined," Jareth said, his eyes scanning the surroundings. "We need to be cautious and rely on the clues we have."

Elara nodded, holding the Box of Foresight tightly. The box had become an invaluable tool, guiding them through the challenges they faced. As they ventured deeper into the glades, the box began to glow faintly, indicating that they were approaching a significant location.

Liora, her sharp eyes constantly on alert, noticed a series of subtle patterns in the foliage that seemed to form a trail. "Look at these markings. They might be a guide to the Hidden Sanctuary."

Following Liora's lead, they navigated through the glades, the patterns in the foliage becoming more distinct. The path led them to a clearing where an ancient stone archway stood, partially covered in vines and moss. The archway was inscribed with runes that glowed with a soft, otherworldly light.

"This must be the entrance," Elara said, her heart quickening with anticipation. "But it seems to be guarded by magic."

Jareth approached the archway and examined the runes. "These runes are designed to test our intentions and worthiness. We need to demonstrate our sincerity and bravery to pass through."

Elara stepped forward, focusing on the runes. She recalled the trials they had faced and the lessons they had learned. Taking a deep breath, she placed her hand on the archway and spoke with conviction. "We seek the Scepter of Valor not for personal gain but to protect the balance and ensure that the power is used for the greater good."

As she spoke, the runes began to glow more brightly, and the archway started to shimmer. The magical barrier protecting the entrance began to dissolve, revealing a hidden passage that led into the heart of the forest.

The passage was dimly lit, with the walls adorned in intricate carvings depicting scenes of valor and heroism. The air was cool and fresh, carrying a sense of ancient wisdom. As they proceeded through the passage, they felt a profound sense of reverence and anticipation.

At the end of the passage, they entered a grand chamber illuminated by the soft glow of bioluminescent crystals embedded in the walls. In the center of the chamber, on a pedestal bathed in ethereal light, stood the Scepter of Valor. The scepter was a magnificent artifact, adorned with symbols of strength and courage, and it radiated a powerful, reassuring energy.

Elara approached the pedestal cautiously. "This is it. The Scepter of Valor."

As she reached out to take the scepter, a sudden rush of wind swept through the chamber, and a figure materialized before them. The figure was an ethereal guardian, its form composed of shimmering light and shadows. The guardian's presence was imposing, and its eyes glowed with a penetrating gaze.

"To claim the Scepter of Valor," the guardian intoned, "you must prove your worthiness through a final trial. You must confront your greatest fears and demonstrate true courage."

The guardian's words resonated deeply, and the chamber began to transform. The walls shifted, and the chamber was filled with scenes of their past fears and regrets—moments of doubt, failure, and loss that had haunted each of them. The trial was not only a test of bravery but a confrontation with their inner demons.

Elara saw visions of her past failures and the weight of responsibility she carried. Jareth faced manifestations of his fears of inadequacy and loss, while Liora confronted her regrets and the burden of past mistakes. The trial forced them to face these fears directly and find the courage to overcome them.

Drawing on their experiences and the strength they had gained from their journey, they faced their fears head-on. Elara found solace in the support of her companions and the knowledge that they had persevered through countless trials together. Jareth and Liora, too, drew strength from their shared mission and the bonds they had forged.

As they confronted and overcame their fears, the chamber began to return to its original form. The guardian's presence softened, and its gaze was filled with approval. "You have proven your worthiness. The Scepter of Valor is yours."

With the guardian's blessing, Elara took the Scepter of Valor from the pedestal. The scepter felt warm and powerful in her hands, its energy resonating with her own. The final artifact was now in their possession, and they had completed the final trial.

The chamber began to shift again, revealing a path that led out of the Hidden Sanctuary. As they emerged from the sanctuary and back into the Whispering Glades, they felt a profound sense of accomplishment and unity.

With the Scepter of Valor in their possession, Elara, Jareth, and Liora prepared to continue their quest. The journey had brought them to this moment of triumph, but they knew that their ultimate goal was still ahead. The power of the artifacts and the wisdom they had gained would guide them as they faced the final challenges and sought to unlock the secrets of the Gate of Aetheria.

As they made their way through the glades, the path to their next destination unfolded before them. The journey had been long and arduous, but they were now more determined than ever to complete their quest and fulfill their mission.

9

The Gathering Storm

The journey had been long, and the final artifacts—the Orb of Insight, the Crown of Harmony, and the Scepter of Valor—were now in the possession of Elara Thornfield, Jareth, and Liora. With these powerful items secured, their quest was nearing its climax. The next step was to unlock the Gate of Aetheria, a monumental task that required not only the artifacts but also a deep understanding of their combined power.

The trio had returned to the heart of the Whispering Glades, where they had set up camp. The air was thick with anticipation and the tension of their impending challenge. The serene beauty of the glades belied the gravity of their mission, and the forest seemed to hold its breath as if awaiting their next move.

Elara sat by the campfire, the artifacts laid out before her. She examined each one carefully, pondering the next steps. The Orb of Insight glowed faintly, the Crown of Harmony rested with an almost imperceptible hum, and the Scepter of Valor emanated a steady, reassuring energy. Together, these artifacts held the key to unlocking the Gate of Aetheria, but the exact process remained elusive.

Jareth and Liora were busy preparing their supplies, their expressions reflecting the weight of their task. Despite their external composure, the magnitude of what lay ahead was evident in their eyes. The sense of urgency grew with each passing moment, as dark clouds gathered on the horizon, signaling the approach of a storm.

"We need to be ready," Jareth said, his voice firm. "The storm could be a sign of the power we're about to unleash or an omen of what's to come."

Liora nodded, her gaze focused on the distant storm clouds. "We should finalize our plan and make sure we understand how to use the artifacts together. The stakes are too high to leave anything to chance."

Elara agreed, and the trio began discussing the final approach. The ancient tome had provided some guidance, but much of the process involved interpreting the artifacts' interactions and aligning them with the gate's mystical properties.

As night fell, the storm drew closer, and the first rumblings of thunder echoed through the glades. The campfire flickered in the growing darkness, casting eerie shadows on the trees. The storm's approach added a layer of urgency to their preparations.

Elara took a deep breath and spoke with determination. "We've come so far, and we've faced many trials together. It's time to use everything we've learned and all the strength we've gained. We need to approach the gate with clarity and resolve."

The storm began to unleash its fury, with lightning flashing across the sky and rain pouring down in sheets. The intensity of the storm mirrored the tension within the trio. Despite the weather's ferocity, they remained focused on their goal, their resolve unwavering.

With their preparations complete, they set out towards the Gate of Aetheria. The storm's rage seemed to intensify as they approached the ancient structure, as if the very elements were responding to their presence.

The gate itself was an imposing, ancient construct, adorned with intricate runes and symbols. Its presence exuded a sense of timeless power and mystery. The artifacts they carried were crucial to unlocking its secrets, but they needed to understand how to align them correctly.

Elara carefully examined the gate, using the Orb of Insight to reveal hidden patterns and clues. The orb's light illuminated the runes, providing insights into the correct arrangement of the artifacts. The Crown of Harmony and the Scepter of Valor were to be placed in specific positions on the gate, while the orb would act as a catalyst to activate its power.

As they worked, the storm's intensity reached a crescendo. The wind howled and lightning illuminated the sky, creating a dramatic and almost apocalyptic backdrop. The energy of the storm seemed to converge on the gate, amplifying its mystical aura.

With everything in place, Elara, Jareth, and Liora took their positions. Elara held the Orb of Insight high, directing its light towards the gate's central symbol. Jareth positioned the Scepter of Valor in its designated slot, and Liora carefully placed the Crown of Harmony on the pedestal.

The gate began to respond to their actions. The runes glowed with an ethereal light, and a low, resonant hum filled the air. The storm's fury seemed to channel into the gate, its energy merging with the artifacts' power.

The trio felt a surge of anticipation as the gate began to open. The storm's energy created a mesmerizing display of light and shadow, casting an otherworldly glow on the gate's surface. The intricate patterns and symbols seemed to come alive, forming a complex tapestry of power and magic.

As the gate fully opened, a swirling vortex of light and energy emerged, revealing a passageway that led to an unknown realm. The storm's intensity began to wane, replaced by a sense of profound stillness and anticipation.

Elara, Jareth, and Liora exchanged determined glances. The Gate of Aetheria had been unlocked, but the path ahead was uncharted and filled with unknown challenges. They were about to embark on the final leg of their journey, and the fate of many worlds rested on their success.

With the storm subsiding and the path revealed, they stepped into the vortex, ready to confront whatever lay beyond the Gate of Aetheria. The gathering storm had been a precursor to their ultimate challenge, and they were prepared to face it with courage and unity.

10

The Realm Beyond

Certainly! Here is a full-text example of Chapter 10 titled "The Realm Beyond":

—-

*The Realm Beyond

The vortex of light and energy enveloped Elara Thornfield, Jareth, and Liora as they stepped through the Gate of Aetheria. The transition was both exhilarating and disorienting, a sensation of being simultaneously weightless and grounded. The swirling colors and shifting patterns of the vortex gave way to a new world as they emerged into a realm unlike any they had seen before.

They found themselves standing in a breathtaking landscape, bathed in a soft, otherworldly light. The sky above was a brilliant tapestry of shifting hues, ranging from deep indigos to shimmering golds. The ground beneath their feet was covered in a delicate, luminescent moss that seemed to pulse gently with each step they took.

The air was filled with the scent of exotic flowers and the sound of a gentle, harmonious melody. Strange, ethereal creatures flitted through the air, their forms translucent and glistening. It was a place of profound beauty and serenity, yet there was an undercurrent of mystery that hinted at deeper challenges.

"This is incredible," Jareth said, his voice filled with awe. "But we must stay focused. The Scepter of Valor's power will be crucial here."

Elara nodded, her eyes scanning the horizon for any signs of the challenges they would face. "We need to find the central nexus of this realm. The final artifact—the Orb of Insight—should guide us."

As they began their exploration, the trio noticed that the realm seemed to shift subtly with each step. Pathways and landmarks appeared to move, making navigation both fascinating and challenging. The harmonious melody they heard was not just a pleasant sound but seemed to be a part of the realm's magic, guiding them through its labyrinthine landscape.

After traversing through mesmerizing forests of crystalline trees and across bridges of light that arched over rivers of liquid stardust, they came upon a grand structure in the distance. It was an imposing tower that reached up into the sky, its spires and turrets adorned with glowing runes.

"That must be the Nexus Tower," Liora suggested. "It looks like it's at the heart of this realm. We should head there."

The journey to the Nexus Tower was both enchanting and treacherous. As they approached, they encountered various magical beings—some friendly and some wary. They were greeted by luminescent guardians who seemed to test their intentions with riddles and challenges. Each encounter required them to use their wisdom and the artifacts they carried.

One guardian, a being of light with eyes like stars, appeared before them. "To pass, you must prove your understanding of balance and unity. Only then can you reach the Nexus Tower."

Elara, drawing on her knowledge and the lessons they had learned, stepped forward. "We have faced many trials and learned the importance of harmony and courage. We seek to restore balance and ensure that the power we obtain is used for the greater good."

The guardian's eyes glowed with approval, and a passageway opened before them, leading directly to the Nexus Tower. The structure was even more magnificent up close, its walls shimmering with intricate patterns of light and energy.

Entering the tower, they were greeted by a vast hall filled with columns of radiant crystal and floors of polished stardust. At the center of the hall stood a pedestal, upon which rested the final artifact: the Heart of Aetheria. The artifact was a pulsating, crystalline orb that radiated a soft, soothing light.

Elara, Jareth, and Liora approached the pedestal, their anticipation palpable. The Heart of Aetheria was the key to harnessing the power of the artifacts and achieving their ultimate goal. As Elara reached out to take it, the air around them shimmered with a sudden burst of energy.

A figure emerged from the shadows of the hall—a guardian of the Nexus Tower, draped in robes of starlight. The guardian's presence was commanding, and their eyes held a deep, ancient wisdom.

"To claim the Heart of Aetheria," the guardian spoke, their voice echoing like a distant chime, "you must demonstrate true unity and resolve. The power of the realm is bound to your intentions and actions."

The final challenge was a test of their collective strength and unity. The room began to transform, presenting them with a series of trials that required them to work together seamlessly. They faced puzzles that tested their intellect, physical challenges that required their combined strength, and moral dilemmas that demanded their highest ideals.

Through each trial, the trio demonstrated their commitment to their mission and to each other. They supported one another, using their individual strengths to overcome obstacles and solve problems. The trials tested their courage, wisdom, and compassion, but they faced each challenge with unwavering determination.

As they completed the final trial, the Heart of Aetheria glowed brightly, and the Nexus Tower's energy stabilized. The guardian's gaze softened, and a sense of calm and approval filled the hall.

"You have proven yourselves worthy," the guardian said. "The Heart of Aetheria is now yours, and the realm is in balance. Use its power wisely, for it holds the key to the harmony of all worlds."

With the Heart of Aetheria in their possession, Elara, Jareth, and Liora felt a profound sense of accomplishment. The realm had tested their resolve and unity, and they had emerged victorious. The final artifact was a symbol of their journey and the culmination of their quest.

As they prepared to leave the realm and return to their world, the Nexus Tower and the surrounding landscape began to fade. The gentle melody of the realm's magic accompanied them as they stepped back through the portal, ready to face the final challenges that awaited them.

With the Heart of Aetheria and their united strength, they were poised to fulfill their mission and restore balance to their world. The journey had brought them to this pivotal moment, and they were prepared to confront the ultimate test with courage and unity.

11

The Final Confrontation

Elara Thornfield, Jareth, and Liora emerged from the portal with the Heart of Aetheria, stepping back into their world. The sky was a tumultuous swirl of dark clouds, reflecting the gravity of their final task. The artifacts were in their possession, but their mission was far from over. The impending storm and the darkening horizon signaled that the final confrontation was imminent.

The path ahead led them to the stronghold of the malevolent force they had been preparing to face—the sorcerer Malakar, who sought to harness the power of the artifacts for his own nefarious purposes. His fortress, known as the Obsidian Citadel, loomed in the distance, its black spires piercing the sky like jagged teeth. The citadel was a fortress of dark magic, and its presence exuded a palpable aura of menace.

As they approached the citadel, the winds howled with an

ominous foreboding, and the temperature seemed to drop. The ground beneath their feet felt unstable, as if the very earth was reacting to their approach. The artifacts they carried pulsed with a sense of urgency, indicating that they were close to their final goal.

"We're almost there," Elara said, her voice resolute. "We need to be prepared for whatever awaits us inside."

Jareth nodded, his grip tightening on his sword. "Malakar will not be easily defeated. We must use the artifacts strategically and rely on our strengths as a team."

Liora, her eyes scanning the surroundings, added, "We should be on high alert. The citadel will be filled with traps and dark magic. We need to move carefully."

As they neared the entrance of the Obsidian Citadel, the grand gates creaked open, revealing a shadowy corridor leading into the heart of the fortress. The air inside was thick with dark magic, and the walls were adorned with eerie, flickering torches that cast unsettling shadows.

The trio advanced cautiously, their steps echoing ominously through the corridors. The citadel was a labyrinth of dark stone and shifting shadows, designed to disorient and deter intruders. The corridors seemed to twist and change, and malevolent forces lurked in the darkness, watching their every move.

Suddenly, the silence was shattered by a deep, resonant voice that seemed to come from every direction at once. "Welcome, heroes. I have been expecting you."

Malakar emerged from the shadows, his form towering and imposing. His eyes glowed with a malevolent fire, and his presence radiated dark energy. He was clad in robes of swirling darkness, and his aura was a palpable force of corruption.

"You dare to challenge me?" Malakar intoned, his voice dripping with disdain. "You think you can thwart my plans with those pitiful artifacts? They are mere toys compared to the power I command."

Elara stepped forward, the Heart of Aetheria held high. "We are here to stop you, Malakar. The power of the artifacts will be used to restore balance and protect the realms. Your reign of darkness ends here."

Malakar's laughter echoed through the citadel, a chilling sound that reverberated off the walls. "You underestimate me, Elara Thornfield. This citadel is my domain, and you are nothing but insects beneath my feet."

With a wave of his hand, Malakar summoned dark creatures from the shadows—twisted, malevolent beings that swarmed towards the trio. The creatures were formidable, their eyes glowing with a sinister light and their forms shifting unnaturally.

Jareth and Liora sprang into action, their weapons and skills coming to the fore. Jareth's sword gleamed with a brilliant light as he cut through the dark creatures, while Liora's arrows struck true, her aim precise and deadly. Elara, holding the Heart of

Aetheria, used its power to create protective barriers and unleash bursts of radiant energy that repelled the dark forces.

Despite their efforts, the battle was fierce. Malakar's dark magic was potent and relentless, and his power seemed to grow stronger with each passing moment. The citadel itself seemed to come alive, its walls shifting and closing in, adding to the chaos of the battle.

As the struggle continued, Elara realized that the key to their victory lay in the combined power of the artifacts. The Orb of Insight, the Crown of Harmony, and the Scepter of Valor needed to be used in concert to counteract Malakar's dark magic and restore balance.

Elara called out to her companions. "We need to combine the artifacts' powers! The Orb of Insight can reveal Malakar's weaknesses, while the Crown of Harmony and the Scepter of Valor can amplify our strength."

Jareth and Liora nodded, understanding the plan. Elara activated the Orb of Insight, its light piercing through the darkness and revealing Malakar's vulnerabilities. The Crown of Harmony was placed upon Elara's head, and the Scepter of Valor was wielded by Jareth, its power amplifying their abilities.

With their combined strength, the trio launched a coordinated assault on Malakar. Elara used the Heart of Aetheria to channel a wave of purifying energy, while Jareth and Liora focused their attacks on Malakar's revealed weaknesses. The forces of light and harmony clashed with the darkness, creating a brilliant and intense struggle.

Malakar roared in frustration as the combined power of the artifacts began to weaken him. His dark magic faltered, and the creatures he had summoned were driven back. The citadel trembled as the balance of power shifted.

In a final, desperate effort, Malakar unleashed a catastrophic burst of dark magic, aiming to destroy everything in his path. Elara, Jareth, and Liora braced themselves, channeling the full power of the artifacts to counteract the attack. The Heart of Aetheria's energy merged with the artifacts' power, creating a powerful shield that repelled Malakar's dark magic.

With a blinding flash of light, the final confrontation reached its climax. Malakar's dark magic was overwhelmed by the combined force of the artifacts, and he was consumed by the light. The citadel's walls crumbled, and the dark presence that had pervaded the fortress was dispelled.

As the dust settled and the darkness receded, the Obsidian Citadel lay in ruins. Elara, Jareth, and Liora stood victorious, their breaths heavy but their spirits lifted. The power of the artifacts had prevailed, and the threat of Malakar was finally vanquished.

The Heart of Aetheria, now glowing with a gentle light, signaled that balance had been restored. The trio stood amidst the ruins of the citadel, their mission accomplished and their world safe once more.

"We did it," Elara said, her voice filled with relief and gratitude. "The darkness has been defeated, and balance has been
restored."

Jareth and Liora nodded in agreement, their expressions reflecting the pride and satisfaction of their achievement. The journey
had been arduous, but their unity and determination had seen
them through.

With the final confrontation behind them, they prepared to
return to their world, ready to rebuild and restore what had been
lost. The artifacts had fulfilled their purpose, and the realm was
once again at peace.

As they left the ruins of the Obsidian Citadel behind, the sky
cleared, and a new dawn began to break. The future was filled
with promise, and their quest had come to a triumphant end.

12

A New Dawn

With the defeat of Malakar and the restoration of balance, Elara Thornfield, Jareth, and Liora emerged from the ruins of the Obsidian Citadel. The once-dark skies had cleared, revealing a brilliant sunrise that bathed the land in a warm, golden light. The world seemed to breathe a sigh of relief, as if celebrating the end of the great conflict that had threatened its very existence.

As they made their way back to their homeland, the trio reflected on the journey that had brought them to this moment. The trials they had faced, the challenges they had overcome, and the bonds they had forged had shaped them into heroes. The artifacts they had wielded were now symbols of their courage and unity.

The journey back was filled with a sense of fulfillment and peace. The landscapes they traversed were vibrant and alive, a testament to the balance that had been restored. The once-tainted lands now flourished with new growth, and the people they encountered greeted them with gratitude and hope.

Upon reaching their homeland, they were met with a heroes' welcome. The people of the realm gathered to celebrate their return, their faces lit with joy and relief. The news of Malakar's defeat and the restoration of balance had spread, and the realm was eager to honor the heroes who had saved it.

In the heart of the capital city, a grand celebration was held in their honor. The streets were adorned with banners and flowers, and music filled the air. The city's leaders, along with citizens from every corner of the realm, gathered to express their gratitude.

Elara, Jareth, and Liora were honored with a ceremonial presentation of medals and titles, recognizing their bravery and sacrifice. The King and Queen, who had watched from a distance, approached to offer their personal thanks.

"Your courage and perseverance have saved our world," the King said, his voice filled with admiration. "You have restored balance and brought hope to our people."

The Queen added, "We are forever grateful for your sacrifice and your commitment to the greater good. You are true heroes, and our realm owes you a debt of gratitude."

Elara, Jareth, and Liora accepted the honors with humility and grace. They were aware that their journey had been a collective effort, supported by the strength of their bond and the wisdom of the artifacts. The recognition was appreciated, but it was the restoration of peace and the well-being of their world that mattered most to them.

As the celebration continued, Elara took a moment to reflect on the journey and the lessons learned. The trials they had faced had taught them the true meaning of courage, unity, and sacrifice. The artifacts had been powerful tools, but it was their unwavering resolve and their trust in one another that had ultimately led to victory.

Jareth and Liora joined Elara on a quiet balcony overlooking the city. The view was breathtaking—a panorama of lush landscapes, bustling streets, and a vibrant sky that seemed to promise a new era.

"We've come a long way," Jareth said, his voice filled with satisfaction. "It's hard to believe it's all over."

Liora nodded, her eyes reflecting the beauty of the scene before them. "We've made a difference. The world is better because of what we've accomplished."

Elara smiled, her heart filled with hope. "The journey may be over, but the future is just beginning. We've restored balance, but it's up to us to ensure that it is maintained and that the lessons we've learned continue to guide us."

The three friends stood together, their hearts united by the shared experience and the promise of a brighter future. The realm had been saved, and a new dawn was rising, filled with opportunities for growth and renewal.

As the sun set on their final day of celebration, Elara, Jareth, and Liora knew that their journey had come full circle. The world was at peace, and they had fulfilled their mission. They were ready to embrace the future, knowing that their actions had made a lasting impact.

The new dawn that greeted them was not just a symbol of the end of their quest but also a reminder of the enduring power of hope and unity. The realm was healed, and the heroes who had saved it were ready to step into the next chapter of their lives.

With hearts full of hope and a sense of accomplishment, Elara, Jareth, and Liora looked towards the horizon. The future was bright, and they were prepared to face it together, knowing that their bond and their courage would continue to guide them in whatever lay ahead.

9 787326 750291